AFFILIATE MARKETING

A BEGINNERS GUIDE

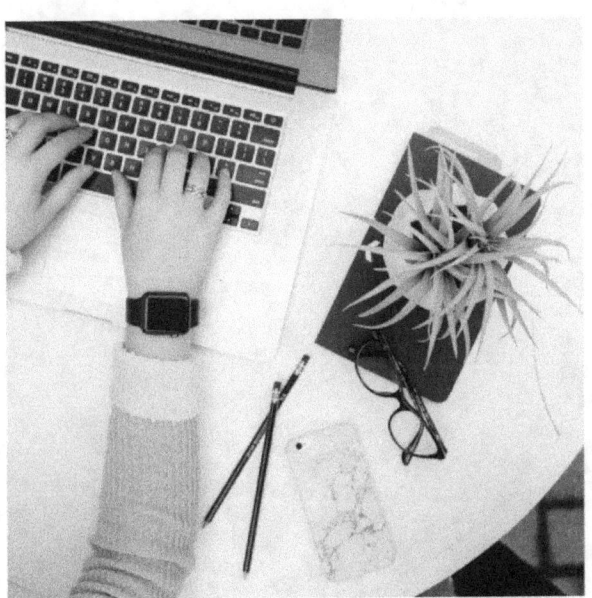

by Will Werhane

Additional Books
By Will Werhane

ANSWERS ABOUT YOUR HOME IN A DIVORCE.
Handling your home sale during a Divorce

EXPIRED!?
A Guide for Selling Homes others couldn't sell. Why your expired doesn't sell and steps to take to get it done.

EARNING THE COMMISSION
Selling by owner. Your Guide to everything that goes into selling FSBO

HOW TO SELL YOUR HOME FOR MORE MONEY
Your guide for getting the most out of a home sale

SELLING AN INHERITED HOUSE
All the steps to sell your inherited home

AFFILIATE MARKETING

A BEGINNERS GUIDE

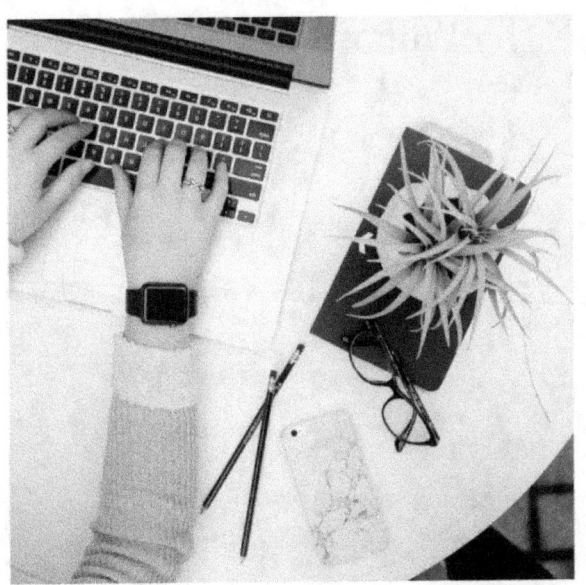

by Will Werhane

Affiliate Marketing

A Beginners Guide

Copyright © 2023

by William L. Werhane

William Werhane
Check my Facebook page https://www.facebook.com/WerhaneW

Printed in the United States of America
ISBN:9798851936456

First Printing July 2023
Published by Kindle Publishing

Dedication

Dedicated to all the hardworking individuals who tirelessly navigate their lives from one paycheck to another, this tribute acknowledges your unwavering determination and resilience. Despite the challenges and uncertainties, your unwavering commitment to your work is truly commendable.

Day after day, you persevere through the demands of your 9-to-5 job, grappling with routine tasks and responsibilities. However, deep within, there may be a burning desire to break free from the monotony to seek a life beyond the confines of conventional employment. This tribute also extends to those who yearn for an escape, who dream of pursuing their passions and carving out their own path.

The journey of living paycheck to paycheck can be arduous, as it often entails financial constraints and limited resources. Yet, it is in these trying circumstances that your resilience shines through. You possess an incredible ability to stretch every dollar, to make ends meet, and to prioritize the needs of your loved ones. Your tenacity in the face of financial hardships is an inspiration to us all.

To those who work paycheck to paycheck and to those who aspire to break free from the constraints of a 9-to-5 job, this tribute serves as a reminder that your dreams are valid and within reach. It encourages you to embrace your passions, to seize opportunities, and to embark on the journey toward a life that aligns with your true aspirations.

Table of Contents

Acknowledgements

I would like to thank my wife, Linda, who has supported me in every one of my endeavors from teaching to entrepreneurship. Her love and support has made it possible for me to escape the 9 to 5 grind.

Welcome to the World of Affiliate Marketing!

If you're interested in starting your own online business, affiliate marketing is a great way to get started. It allows you to promote products and services from other businesses and earn commissions on sales that you refer. And the best part? You don't have to worry about creating your own products or handling customer service.

But, like any business, affiliate marketing requires knowledge and effort to succeed. That's why this book is here to guide you through the process. You'll learn how to find a profitable niche, choose the right affiliate programs, create high-quality content, promote your offers, and track your results.

In this book, you'll also learn the importance of building relationships with merchants and customers, avoiding common mistakes, and scaling your business for long-term success. Plus, we'll cover the benefits of becoming an affiliate marketer and the next steps you can take to get started.

Whether you're a complete beginner or have some experience in online marketing, this book will provide you with the tools and knowledge you need to build a successful affiliate marketing business. So, let's get started!

Chapter 1

Understanding Affiliate Marketing

Definition of Affiliate Marketing

Affiliate marketing is a form of performance-based marketing where businesses reward affiliates for promoting their products or services. Affiliates promote the products or services to their audience and receive a commission for each lead or sale generated through their unique affiliate link. It is a mutually beneficial arrangement between the merchant (the business offering the product or service) and the affiliate (the individual or entity promoting the product or service). Affiliate marketing is an ever-expanding way for companies to increase their sales and for individuals to earn passive income online.

How Affiliate Marketing Works

Affiliate marketing works through a partnership between a merchant and an affiliate. The merchant offers products or services for sale, and the affiliate promotes them to their audience. The affiliate is provided with a unique link or code that tracks any sales or leads generated through their efforts.

Here are the general steps of how affiliate marketing works:

The merchant creates an affiliate program and provides marketing materials such as banners, links, and other assets to help affiliates promote their products or services.

The affiliate joins the merchant's affiliate program. They receive a unique affiliate link or code to promote the merchant's products or services.

The affiliate promotes the services or products through multiple platforms such as blogging, social media, email marketing, or their own website.

When a customer clicks on the affiliate's unique link or uses their unique code to make a purchase or complete a desired action, such as filling out a form, the merchant's system tracks the sale or lead generated through the affiliate's efforts.

The merchant then pays the affiliate a percentage of the sale or a commission, as agreed upon in the affiliate program terms.

The affiliate can then track their earnings and performance through the merchant's affiliate dashboard.

This process benefits both the merchant and the affiliate. The merchant can increase their sales and reach a larger audience through the affiliate's promotion efforts. The affiliate can earn passive income by promoting products or services they believe to their audience.

Some forms of Affiliate Marketing Programs are:

There are many types of affiliate marketing programs available to affiliates. Some of the most common types are:

Pay-Per-Sale (PPS): Pay-per-sale affiliate programs are the most common type of affiliate marketing program. Affiliates are paid a commission for every sale they generate through their unique affiliate link.

Pay-Per-Click (PPC): Pay-per-click affiliate programs pay affiliates for every click on their unique affiliate link. This type of program is less common, as tracking clicks and ensuring they are legitimate can be more difficult.

Pay-Per-Lead (PPL): Pay-per-lead affiliate programs pay affiliates for every lead they generate through their unique affiliate link. This could be a sign-up for a free trial, a subscription to a newsletter, or any other desired action.

Two-Tier: Two-tier affiliate programs offer affiliates the opportunity to earn commissions on their own sales and also on the sales generated from affiliates they refer to the program.

Multi-Level Marketing (MLM): Multi-level marketing programs are similar to two-tier programs. However, they also allow affiliates to earn commissions on the sales generated by affiliates they refer to and those referred by those affiliates. This creates a hierarchical structure with multiple levels of affiliates.

Cost-Per-Action (CPA): Cost-per-action affiliate programs pay affiliates a commission for specific actions, such as filling out a form, downloading an app, or watching a video.

Subscription: Subscription affiliate programs pay affiliates a commission for every subscription or recurring payment made by a customer referred through their unique affiliate link.

Researching and evaluating affiliate programs carefully before joining is essential to ensure that they align with your niche and goals as an affiliate marketer.

Benefits of Affiliate Marketing for Businesses and Affiliates

Affiliate marketing offers benefits to both businesses and affiliates. Here are some of the key benefits:

Benefits for Businesses:

Cost-Effective: Affiliate marketing is a performance-based marketing model. Businesses only pay commissions when an affiliate's efforts generate a sale or lead. This makes it a cost-effective way for businesses to promote their products or services.

Increased Reach: Affiliates can promote a business's products or services to their own audience, which can help companies to reach a wider audience and expand their customer base.

Targeted Marketing: Affiliates often have a niche audience that aligns with a business's target market, meaning companies can benefit from highly targeted marketing efforts.

Brand Awareness: Affiliate marketing can increase a business's brand awareness through exposure to new audiences and increased visibility on affiliate websites and social media channels.

Low Risk: Affiliate marketing is a low-risk marketing strategy for businesses, as they only pay commissions for actual sales or leads generated through affiliate efforts.

Benefits for Affiliates:

Passive Income: Affiliate marketing allows affiliates to earn income passively by promoting products or services to their audience.

Low Start-up Costs: Affiliate marketing requires minimal start-up costs, as affiliates can promote products or services through their own website or social media channels.

Flexible Schedule: Affiliate marketing offers the flexibility to work from home or anywhere and at any time, which makes it an ideal choice for individuals who want to work from home or on a part-time basis.

No Inventory Management: Affiliates don't have to worry about inventory management or order fulfillment, as the business handles these tasks.

Opportunity for Growth: Successful affiliates can earn a significant income through affiliate marketing and may even have the opportunity to grow their business and become full-time affiliate marketers.

Affiliate marketing offers numerous benefits for businesses and affiliates, making it a popular and effective marketing strategy.

Conclusion

In conclusion, affiliate marketing is a powerful marketing strategy allowing businesses to expand their reach and increase sales through the efforts of affiliates who promote their products or services. It offers a cost-effective, low-risk way for businesses to market their products or services and reach new audiences.

For affiliates, affiliate marketing offers the opportunity to earn income passively by promoting products or services they believe to their audience. It requires minimal start-up costs and provides a flexible schedule, making it an ideal choice for individuals who want to work from home or on a part-time basis.

Multiple affiliate marketing programs are available, including pay-per-sale, pay-per-click, pay-per-lead, two-tier, multi-level marketing, cost-per-action, and subscription. It's essential for both businesses and affiliates to carefully evaluate affiliate programs before joining to ensure that they align with their niche and goals.

Overall, affiliate marketing is a win-win strategy for both businesses and affiliates, and it's a proven marketing method that has helped many businesses increase their revenue and grow their customer base.

Chapter 2

Finding a Niche

Why Choosing a Niche is Important

Choosing a niche is essential for several reasons when it comes to affiliate marketing. These are some of the key reasons why:

Targeted Marketing: By choosing a niche, you can laser focus your marketing efforts on a specific group of people most likely to be interested in the products or services you promote. This allows you to create more targeted and effective marketing campaigns.

Authority and Expertise: Focusing on a specific niche allows you to become an authority within that niche and build your expertise. Doing this can help you gain credibility and trust with your audience, making them more likely to purchase products or services you recommend.

Better Conversion Rates: By targeting a specific audience, you can create content and promotions that are tailored to their needs and interests. Target marketing can result in higher conversion rates, as your audience is more likely to be interested in and purchase the products or services you promote.

Less Competition: Choosing a niche helps you stand out in a jam-packed marketplace by offering a unique perspective and catering to a specific audience. This can help you extricate yourself from competitors and attract a loyal audience.

Greater Profitability: Focusing on a specific niche can help you identify high-ticket or high-demand products or services that can be more profitable. You can increase your earnings potential by promoting these products or services to a targeted audience.

Therefore, choosing a niche is an essential aspect of affiliate marketing that can help you build credibility, increase conversion rates, and achieve greater profitability. It allows you to focus your marketing efforts on a specific audience and create targeted campaigns that reverberate with your audience, making it more likely that they will purchase the products or services you promote.

How to Choose a Profitable Niche

Choosing a profitable niche is a critical factor in the success of your affiliate marketing efforts. These are some steps to help you choose a profitable niche:

Identify your Interests: Start by brainstorming topics or areas you are interested in or passionate about. This will make it simpler for you to create content and promote products that you are knowledgeable about and enjoy.

Research the Demand: Use keyword research tools like Google Keyword Planner or Ubersuggest to identify topics with high search volume and low competition. This will help you identify niches that are in demand but not oversaturated with competition.

Analyze the Competition: Check out your potential competitors' websites and social media channels to see what they are doing well and where there may be gaps in the market. This will help you analyze opportunities to differentiate yourself and offer a unique perspective.

Consider Profitability: Evaluate the potential profitability of your niche by researching the average commission rates for products or services in that niche. Consider the price point of products or services in that niche and whether they offer high-ticket or recurring commissions.

Test and Iterate: Once you have chosen a niche, begin creating content and promoting products, then see what resonates with your target market. Monitor your results, then adjust your strategy as needed to optimize your profitability.

It is important to note that choosing a profitable niche is not a one-time decision but rather an ongoing process. As the market and trends change, you may need to adjust your strategy and pivot to new niches to maintain your profitability. By staying informed and adapting to changes in the market, you can continue to grow and succeed as an affiliate marketer.

How to Research your Niche

Researching your niche is an essential step in the affiliate marketing process. It allows you to identify key trends, understand your audience, and stay up-to-date with industry developments. Here are some steps to help you research your niche:

Identify your Audience: Determining your target audience and their needs and interests. This will help you create content and promotions tailored to their needs and resonate with them.

Check out Industry Publications: Look for industry publications, blogs, and newsletters that cover your niche. This will help you stay up-to-date with the latest trends and developments in your niche and identify potential promotional opportunities.

Use Keyword Research Tools: Use keyword research tools like Google Keyword Planner or Ubersuggest to identify topics and popular search terms related to your niche. This will help you identify potential topics to write about and create content about.

Check out Social Media: Look for social media groups and communities related to your niche. This will give you insight into what your target audience is talking about and their pain points and challenges.

Analyze your Competitors: Look at your competitors' websites and social media channels to see what types of content and promotions are working well for them. This will help you identify gaps in the market and opportunities to differentiate yourself.

Monitor Industry Events and Conferences: Attend industry events and conferences related to your niche to stay up-to-date with the latest developments and trends. This can also be an excellent opportunity to network with others in your industry and build relationships.

Collect Data and Analyze it: Use tools like Google Analytics to track the performance of your website and social media channels. Stepping back to analyze your results will help you identify which types of content and promotions resonate with your audience and which are not.

By taking the time to research your niche, your understanding of your target audience comes into focus, you stay up-to-date with industry trends, and you identify potential opportunities for growth and profitability.

Conclusion

Finding a niche is a crucial step in starting your affiliate marketing journey. By selecting a profitable niche, you can focus on promoting products with high demand and a willing audience. Researching your niche thoroughly, understanding your target audience, and keeping up with industry trends are essential. By following these steps, you can increase your chances of success in affiliate marketing and achieve your goals. Remember, selecting a niche is just the beginning of your journey, and it is essential to continue learning and adapting to the evolving market to ensure long-term success.

Chapter 3

Finding Affiliate Programs

Different ways to Find Affiliate Programs

There are several ways to find affiliate programs to join. These are but a few of the most common methods:

Search Engines: Use search engines like Google or Bing to search for affiliate programs related to your niche. For example, if your niche is fitness, you could search for "fitness affiliate programs" or "fitness product affiliate programs."

Affiliate Networks: Affiliate networks are platforms connecting affiliates with merchants who offer affiliate programs. Some popular affiliate networks include Commission Junction, ShareASale, and Rakuten Marketing.

Product or Service Websites: Check the websites of products or services related to your niche to see if they offer affiliate programs. Many companies will have an "Affiliate" or "Partner" program link in their website footer or menu.

Social Media: Follow brands and influencers in your niche on social media to see if they promote affiliate programs. You can use hashtags to search for products related to your niche to find potential opportunities.

Competitor Websites: Look at your competitor's websites to see if they promote affiliate programs. This can be an excellent way to identify potential opportunities and see what types of products or services are popular in your niche.

Affiliate Program Directories: Many directories list affiliate programs by niche. Some popular directories include AffiliatePrograms.com and AffiliateSeeking.com.

Industry Events: Attend industry events and conferences related to your niche to meet potential affiliate partners and network with other experts in your industry.

By combining these methods, you can find a cross-section of affiliate programs to choose from and identify the ones that best fit your audience and promotional strategy.

Types of Affiliate Programs

There are several types of affiliate programs, each with its own structure and commission model. Here is a smattering of the most prevalent types:

Pay-Per-Sale (PPS): This is the most common type of affiliate program. With a PPS program, affiliates earn a commission for each sale they generate for the merchant. Commissions are typically a percentage of the sale amount, ranging from 5% to 50% or more.

Pay-Per-Click (PPC): With a PPC program, affiliates earn a commission for each click on an affiliate link. Whether a sale is made or not. PPC programs are less common than PPS programs and typically offer lower commission rates.

Pay-Per-Lead (PPL): With a PPL program, an affiliate earns a commission for each lead they generate for the merchant. A lead is typically defined as a completed form or other action that indicates interest in the merchant's products or services.

Two-Tier: A two-tier program allows affiliates to earn commissions not only on their sales or leads but also on the sales or leads generated by affiliates they refer to the program.

Multi-Tier: A multi-tier program allows affiliates to earn commissions not only on their sales or leads and the sales or leads generated by affiliates they refer to the program but also on the sales or leads generated by affiliates those referrals generate and so on.

Recurring Commissions: Affiliate programs offer recurring commissions, which means affiliates earn a commission for every recurring payment made by the customer they refer. This is common in subscription-based services.

Influencer Programs: Some merchants offer influencer programs, which are specifically designed for social media influencers. These programs typically provide unique commission structures and promotional materials tailored to the influencer's brand and audience.

By understanding the different types of affiliate programs, you can determine the one that best fits your promotional strategy and audience and maximize your earning potential as an affiliate marketer.

How to Evaluate Affiliate Programs

When evaluating affiliate programs, several factors must be considered to determine if it is a good fit for you and your audience. Here are some key things to look for:

Commission Rate: The commission rate is a percentage of the sale that the affiliate will earn. Look for programs with competitive commission rates that will make it worth your time and effort to promote their products or services.

Cookie Duration: The cookie duration is the amount of time that a visitor has to make the purchase after clicking on your affiliate link for you to earn a commission. Longer cookie durations are better because they increase the likelihood of earning a commission on a sale.

Conversion Rate: The conversion rate is a percentage of visitors who click on your affiliate link and make a purchase. Look for programs with high conversion rates, indicating that the merchant's products or services are popular and in demand.

Product Quality: Promoting products or services that are high quality and relevant to your audience is essential. Making sure the merchant's products or services are an excellent fit for your niche and audience is critical.

Merchant Reputation: Look for affiliate programs offered by reputable merchants with a track record of treating affiliates well and paying commissions on time.

Affiliate Support: Look for programs that offer good affiliate support, such as access to promotional materials, dedicated account managers, and responsive customer support.

Payment Terms: Check the payment terms of the program, including how often payments are made and what payment methods are available.

By considering these factors, you can evaluate affiliate programs and choose the ones that are the best fit for you and your audience and offer the highest earning potential.

Affiliate Networks

Affiliate networks are platforms that connect merchants with affiliates. They offer a spectrum of benefits for both parties, including access to a larger pool of potential partners and streamlined management and tracking of affiliate programs.

Here are some of the top affiliate networks:

Amazon Associates: This affiliate program is one of the biggest and most popular in the world. It offers a wide range of products to promote and a commission structure that rewards high-performing affiliates.

Commission Junction: Commission Junction (CJ) is a popular affiliate network offering various programs across various niches. It provides advanced tracking and reporting tools and access to a large pool of advertisers.

ShareASale: ShareASale is another prominent affiliate network with over 4,500 merchants in a variety of niches. It offers advanced tracking and reporting tools and a range of promotional materials and resources for affiliates.

Rakuten Marketing: Rakuten Marketing is a worldwide affiliate network with over 1,000 advertisers across various industries. It offers advanced tracking and reporting tools and a range of promotional materials and resources for affiliates.

ClickBank: ClickBank is a popular affiliate network specializing in digital products like e-books and online courses. It offers high commission rates and advanced tracking and reporting tools.

FlexOffers: FlexOffers is another affiliate network that offers a wide range of programs across various niches, including health and wellness, finance, and technology. It provides advanced tracking and reporting tools and a range of promotional materials and resources for affiliates.

By joining an affiliate network, you can access a wide range of programs and merchants, advanced tracking and reporting tools, promotional materials, and support. This can help you maximize your earning potential as an affiliate marketer.

Conclusion

In conclusion, finding suitable affiliate programs is a crucial aspect of affiliate marketing. Affiliate marketers can use various methods to find relevant affiliate programs, such as conducting online searches, checking affiliate networks, and exploring different types of affiliate programs. Evaluating an affiliate program based on several factors, such as commission rates, product quality, and merchant credibility, is essential. Additionally, affiliate networks provide a valuable platform for discovering and joining multiple affiliate programs. By carefully selecting the right affiliate programs, marketers can increase their chances of success and earn more significant profits.

Chapter 4

Building a Website

Why you need a Website as an Affiliate Marketer

As an affiliate marketer, having a website is crucial for several reasons:

Authority: A website gives you a platform to establish your expertise and authority in your niche. By sharing high-quality content, reviews, and recommendations, you can build trust with your audience and become a go-to resource for information and guidance.

Branding: A website allows you to create a solid and unforgettable brand that resonates with your audience. A website is a tool to showcase your unique value proposition and separate yourself from other affiliates in your niche.

Traffic Generation: A website allows you to drive traffic to your affiliate offers through various channels, such as search engines, social media, and email marketing. Optimizing your website for search engines and providing high-quality content can attract targeted traffic that is more inclined to convert into sales.

Tracking and Optimization: A website allows you to track your traffic and conversion data, which can help you optimize your affiliate campaigns for maximum profitability. You can use analytics tools to identify which offers and promotions perform best and adjust accordingly.

Compliance: Some affiliate programs require affiliates to have a website to participate. Having a website can ensure that you meet the program's requirements and avoid any potential compliance issues.

Overall, a website is an essential tool for affiliate marketers who want to build a successful and sustainable business. It allows you to establish authority, drive targeted traffic, and optimize your campaigns for maximum profitability.

How to Choose a Domain Name

Choosing the right domain name is essential because it will be the foundation of your online presence. Here are some tips for choosing a domain name for your affiliate marketing website:

Make it Memorable: Your domain name must be easy to remember and spell. Avoid using numbers or hyphens, as they make it more difficult for users to remember.

Keep it Concise: A shorter domain name is more likely to be remembered and more likely to be typed (or entered) correctly. Aim for a name that is less than 15 characters.

Choose a Relevant Name: Your domain name should reflect the focus of your website and the niche you are targeting. This will help users understand what your website is about and make it more feasible that they will visit and engage with your content.

Make it Brandable: A brandable domain name is unique and memorable and can help you stand out in a crowded niche. Consider using a made-up word or combining two relevant words to create a unique and memorable name.

Check for Availability: When choosing a domain name, ensure it is available. You can use a domain registrar or hosting service to check availability and purchase your domain name.

Consider SEO: While it's not necessary to include keywords in your domain name, it can help with search engine optimization (SEO). Consider having relevant keywords in your domain name while maintaining its memorability and brand appeal.

Avoid Trademark Issues: Verify that your domain name does not infringe on trademarks or copyrights. You can search for trademarks using the US Patent and Trademark Office's website or a similar service in your country.

Choosing a domain name is an important decision that requires careful consideration. By following these tips, you can choose a memorable, relevant, and brandable domain name that helps you build a solid online presence.

Choosing a Hosting Provider

Selecting the appropriate hosting provider is essential for ensuring the triumph of your affiliate marketing website. Here are some aspects to consider when choosing a hosting provider:

Reliability and Uptime: Your website should be available to visitors around the clock. Look for a hosting provider with a reliable uptime guarantee of at least 99%.

Speed and Performance: Website speed is a critical factor in user experience and search engine optimization. Choosing a hosting provider with fast load times and optimized server performance is imperative.

Customer Support: Look for a hosting provider with responsive and knowledgeable customer support. You should be able to get help quickly and efficiently if you run into technical issues or have questions about your hosting service.

Scalability: As your website grows and engages more traffic, your current hosting plan may need to be upgraded to accommodate increased demand. Search for a hosting provider that offers flexible and scalable hosting plans.

Security: Your website and data should be secure and protected from cyber threats. Look for a hosting provider with powerful and powerful security features, such as SSL certificates, firewalls, and regular backups.

Price and Value: Compare hosting providers based on their pricing and the value they offer. Consider the features included in each plan and any additional fees for add-ons or upgrades.

User interface and ease of use: Your hosting provider should have a user-friendly interface and easy-to-use tools for managing your website and hosting account.

Some popular affiliate-market hosting providers include Bluehost, SiteGround, HostGator, and WP Engine. Be sure to research and compare providers based on your specific needs and budget before making your decision.

Building a Website using WordPress

WordPress is a popular and user-friendly platform for building websites, including affiliate marketing websites. Here are the basic steps for building a website using WordPress:

Choose a Domain Name and Hosting Provider: You'll need a domain name and hosting service before building your website. Follow my earlier tips for choosing a domain name and hosting provider.

Install WordPress: All most all hosting providers offer a one-click installation of WordPress, making it quick and easy to get started. Once you've installed WordPress, you can log in to your website's dashboard.

Choose a Theme: A theme determines the look and feel of your website. Choose a theme relevant to your niche and offers the features and customization options you need.

Install Plugins: Plugins add functionality to your website. Some essential plugins for affiliate marketing websites include an SEO plugin, a caching plugin, and a security plugin. Choose plugins based on your specific needs.

Create Pages and Posts: Pages are used for static content, such as your About page and contact page. Posts are used for blog content and product reviews. Create pages and posts using the WordPress editor.

Add Affiliate Links: You can add affiliate links to your website's content using text links or banners. Use an affiliate link management plugin to track clicks and earnings.

Optimize for SEO: SEO is essential for driving traffic to your website. Use an SEO plugin to optimize your content for search engines, including using relevant keywords, meta descriptions, and title tags.

Test and Launch: Once you've created your website and added content, test it thoroughly to make sure everything is working correctly. Then, launch your website and start promoting it to your audience.

Building a website using WordPress can be relatively simple, especially with the availability of pre-made themes and plugins. However, investing time and effort into creating high-quality content and optimizing your website for SEO to attract and engage visitors is crucial.

Setting up your Website

Setting up your website involves several steps, including:

Choose a Domain Name and Hosting Provider: Make sure you choose a domain name that reflects your niche and is effortless to remember. Consider a hosting provider that offers fast loading speeds, reliable uptime, and responsive customer support.

Install WordPress: Most hosting providers offer one-click installations of WordPress, making it easy to get started. Log in to your website's dashboard to begin customizing your site.

Choose a Theme: Choose a theme that is relevant to your niche and offers the features and customization options you need. You can find free and premium themes on WordPress.org or from third-party developers.

Customize Your Theme: Customize your theme's colors, fonts, layout, and other elements to match your branding and create a cohesive look and feel.

Install Plugins: Install plugins that add functionality to your website, such as an SEO plugin, a caching plugin, and a security plugin.

Create Pages and Posts: Create pages for static content, such as your "about page" and "contact page", and create posts for blog content and product reviews.

Add Affiliate Links: Add affiliate links to your content using text links or banners. Use an affiliate link management plugin to track clicks and earnings.

Optimize for SEO: Optimize all your content for search engines, including using relevant keywords, meta descriptions, and title tags.

Test and Launch: Test your website thoroughly to ensure everything works correctly before launching it to the public. Consider getting feedback from friends or family to improve your site before promoting it to a broader audience.

Setting up your website is a crucial step in becoming an affiliate marketer. It's essential to take the time to customize your site and create high-quality content that engages your target market and drives traffic to your affiliate links.

Conclusion

In conclusion, building a website is essential in starting your affiliate marketing journey. It provides a platform to showcase your chosen niche and promote relevant affiliate products to your audience. To build a website, you must select a domain name and hosting provider, then create and set up your website using WordPress or other website builders. Establishing a website creates a professional online image. Which helps gain credibility and trust from potential customers.

Chapter 5

Creating Content

Content is crucial for affiliate marketing because it helps you attract and engage your audience. When people visit your website, they seek information and provide users with answers to their inquiries and solutions to their issues. By providing valuable, high-quality content that addresses these needs, you can establish yourself as an authority in your niche and earn the trust of your audience.

Why Content is Essential for Affiliate Marketing

Content is crucial for affiliate marketing because it helps you attract and engage your audience. Visitors who visit your website seek information, answers to their inquiries, and solutions to their issues. Offering valuable content that meets the needs of your audience is crucial to gaining their trust, thus establishing yourself as an expert in your niche. This can be achieved by providing high-quality content.

Here are some specific reasons why content is vital for affiliate marketing:

Drives Traffic: High-quality content optimized for search engines can help drive traffic to your website. To increase traffic to your website, focus on using relevant keywords, providing answers to common search queries, and developing content that people will want to share.

Builds Trust: By offering valuable and relevant content that caters to your audience's interests, you can establish trust with your readers. This trust is crucial for affiliate marketing because people are more likely to buy from someone they trust.

Positions You as an Authority: Establishing yourself as an expert in your field can be achieved effectively by creating top-notch content highlighting your skills and knowledge. The ability to do this lies in your hands. Take charge and assert your expertise. You can show others that you are a force to be reckoned with. This can help you attract more readers, build a following, and become your audience's trusted source of information.

Generates Leads: High-quality content that provides value to your audience can also help you generate leads. You can capture your readers' contact information and build your email list by offering free resources, such as eBooks or email courses.

Increases Conversions: If you produce content that informs, engages, and is relevant to your audience, it is more probable they will click on your affiliate links and buy something. To boost your affiliate commissions, it is possible to enhance your conversions. by providing valuable information and helping your audience find the solutions they need.

In short, content is the backbone of affiliate marketing, and it helps attract and engage your audience, build trust and credibility, and increase conversions and earnings.

Different Types of Content

There are several types of content that you can create as an affiliate marketer to engage your audience, build trust, and promote your affiliate products. To help you better understand, here are some of the most frequently encountered types of content:

Blog Posts: Blogging is a great way to create high-quality, informative content that attracts traffic to your website. To establish your expertise in your niche and advertise your affiliate products, write blog posts catering to your audience's interests and requirements.

Product Reviews: Writing product reviews effectively showcases your niche knowledge and promotes your affiliate products. By providing honest, unbiased reviews of the products you promote, you can help your audience make informed purchasing decisions.

How-to Guides and Tutorials: Creating how-to guides and tutorials is a great way to provide value to your audience and position yourself as an expert in your niche. One way to gain the trust of your audience and advertise your affiliate products is by sharing your knowledge and expertise. This can help establish credibility and encourage potential customers to make a purchase.

Videos: Using video content is a growing trend that can effectively attract and engage your audience while promoting your affiliate products. You can create videos showcasing your products, provide tutorials, or share your experiences and insights.

Infographics: Using infographics is an effective method of presenting information in an attractive and easy-to-understand manner. By creating infographics summarizing information or providing insights into your niche, you can attract and engage your audience and promote your affiliate products.

EBooks and Whitepapers: Creating eBooks and whitepapers is a great way to provide value to your audience and capture leads. You can expand your email list and market your affiliate products by providing free resources catering to your audience's preferences and requirements.

These are but a few examples of the types of content you can create as an affiliate marketer. The key is to create content that provides value to your audience and promotes your affiliate products naturally and authentically.

How to Create High-Quality Content

Creating high-quality content is essential for building trust with your audience and promoting your affiliate products effectively. Here are some tips for creating high-quality content:

Identify Your Audience: Before creating content, it is essential to identify your audience and understand their needs, interests, and pain points. Creating content that speaks directly to your audience can increase engagement and build trust.

Research Your Topic: To create high-quality content, you must be well informed about your niche. Dedicating sufficient time to conducting thorough research on your chosen topic is crucial, and using reputable sources and staying up-to-date on the latest developments and trends is imperative.

Use a Clear Structure: When creating content, it's essential to use a straightforward format that makes it easy for your audience to read and understand. To enhance the readability of your content, consider implementing subheadings, bullet points, and other formatting techniques to divide it into smaller sections.

Provide Value: Your content should provide value to your audience by addressing their needs and answering their questions. Whether you're writing a blog post, creating a tutorial, or filming a video, ensure your content is informative, engaging, and relevant.

Use Visuals: Visuals can help break up your content and make it more engaging. Consider using images, videos, infographics, and other visual elements to enhance your content and make it more appealing to your audience.

Write in a Conversational Tone: Using a conversational tone can establish a connection with your audience and develop trust. To ensure maximum readability and comprehension, avoid complex language and jargon. Your content should be easily understood by all, so keep it simple.

Edit and Proofread: Before publishing your content, edit and proofread it carefully. To ensure the quality of your content, check for any spelling and grammar errors and ensure that your writing flows smoothly. It is imperative that any necessary revisions are made to your content to guarantee its high quality and error-free status. Avoid altering the meaning of the text, adding any new information, sentences, or paragraphs, or removing any essential information. Ensure that the same level of formality is maintained in the rewrite as in the original text.

Producing top-notch content requires dedication and hard work. But it's essential for building trust with your audience and promoting your affiliate products effectively. By following these tips, you can create content that engages your audience, provides value, and promotes your affiliate products naturally and authentically.

Keyword Research and SEO

Keyword research involves identifying specific words. and phrases people use to search for information online. It is an essential part of SEO or search engine optimization; it can assist you in determining what your intended audience is searching for and provide recommendations on how to enhance your content to improve your search engine ranking.in search engine results pages (SERPs).

Here are some steps to perform keyword research for your affiliate marketing website:

Identify Your Niche: To start, you must identify your niche and understand the specific topics, products, or services you want to promote. This will help you identify the right keywords for your content.

Brainstorm Keyword Ideas: Begin by brainstorming a list of keywords and phrases related to your niche. Use a tool like Google's Keyword Planner, Ubersuggest, or SEMrush to generate a list of potential keywords.

Analyze Search Intent: Understanding the meaning behind your chosen keywords is essential. Are people looking for information, products, or services? Use search engines to analyze the top-ranking pages for each keyword and determine what kind of content best matches the search intent.

Evaluate Keyword Competition: Use a keyword research tool to analyze the competition for each keyword. Look for keywords with high search volume and low competition to optimize your chances of ranking higher in search results.

Optimize Your Content: After determining the identification, and correct keywords, optimizing your content to rank higher in search results is crucial. Include the keywords in your content, titles, meta descriptions, and other elements of your website, helping search engines comprehend your content's subject matter.

Driving traffic to your affiliate marketing website and promoting your products effectively is essential, but it requires ongoing time and effort in the form of SEO. By performing keyword research and optimizing your content, you can increase your chances of ranking higher in search results and attracting more visitors to your website.

Conclusion

In summary, content is a critical aspect of affiliate marketing. It allows you to effectively communicate with your audience, build trust, and promote products. By creating high-quality content, you can engage your audience and encourage them to take action, such as clicking on your affiliate links and making a purchase.

You can create various types of content, such as blog posts, product reviews, videos, podcasts, and social media posts. Each type of content has advantages, and it's important to experiment with different formats to see what resonates with your audience.

Producing superior content demands dedication and effort, but the payoff is ultimately significant. To create compelling content, you must understand your audience, provide value, and use a clear and engaging tone. Optimizing your content for search engines by performing keyword research and implementing SEO best practices is essential.

By following these steps, you can create compelling and effective content that drives traffic to your website, promotes your products, and generates affiliate revenue. To succeed in affiliate marketing, focus on providing value to your audience and building a relationship based on trust and transparency.

Chapter 6

Promoting Affiliate Products

Different ways to Promote Affiliate Products

To effectively promote affiliate products, trying out different strategies that resonate with your specific audience and niche is essential. Here are some of the most popular techniques for promoting affiliate products:

Blogging: Blogging is a popular way to promote affiliate products, and it allows you to create long-form content that can rank well in search engines. You can write product reviews, comparison posts, "how-to" guides, and other content promoting your affiliate links.

Social Media: If you have a large and engaged following on social media platforms like Instagram, Facebook, and Twitter, you can effectively promote affiliate products. You can share product photos, reviews, and other content encouraging your audience to click on your affiliate links.

Email Marketing: One effective method to advertise affiliate products to your subscribers is through email marketing. You can send out regular newsletters, product reviews, and promotions that include your affiliate links.

YouTube: A popular platform for creating product reviews, tutorials, and other content types promoting affiliate products. To monetize your YouTube videos, you can either add affiliate links to the video description or utilize YouTube's YouTube Partner Program, which has an affiliate program built-in.

Paid Advertising: Utilizing paid advertising can prove to be a successful strategy to promote affiliate products, especially if you have a budget for advertising. To reach specific audiences and promote your affiliate links, consider utilizing platforms such as Google Ads, Facebook Ads, or Instagram Ads.

Webinars: One effective method to market affiliate products to a specific audience is hosting webinars. You can create educational webinars that promote your affiliate products and provide value to your audience.

These are only a few examples among the numerous one's available ways to promote affiliate products. The key is experimenting with different strategies and finding what works best for your audience and niche. Remember, the most effective affiliate promotions provide value to your audience and build trust and credibility over time.

How to Create an Effective Affiliate Marketing Strategy

You must clearly understand your target audience, niche, and goals to create an effective affiliate marketing strategy. Here are some steps that can assist you in creating an effective affiliate marketing strategy:

Define your Niche and audience: As we have discussed earlier, choosing a niche is essential. You need to identify the specific audience you want to target, their interests, pain points, and needs. By implementing this strategy, you can create content that connects with your audience and highlights useful and relevant products.

Choose the right Affiliate Programs: Choosing the right affiliate programs is crucial for the success of your affiliate marketing strategy. You must evaluate the affiliate programs you want to promote and ensure they align with your niche and audience.

Create High-Quality Content: As discussed earlier, creating high-quality content is essential for promoting affiliate products effectively. You must create informative, engaging, and valuable content for your audience. This will help you build trust and credibility with your audience, which in turn will increase your affiliate revenue.

Optimize your Content for SEO: Keyword research and SEO are essential components of an effective affiliate marketing strategy. Optimizing your content for search engines by implementing effective strategies, you can increase your website traffic and improve your chances of making sales.

Build an Email List: Email marketing is a powerful tool for promoting affiliate products. By building an email list, you can communicate with your audience directly and promote relevant affiliate products.

Track Your Results: To evaluate the effectiveness of your affiliate marketing strategy, you need to track your results. Analytics tools enable monitoring your website traffic, click-through rates, and conversions. This will assist you in recognizing what is effective and what is not, allowing you to adjust your strategy as necessary.

Experiment with Different Strategies: Trying out various affiliate marketing tactics is paramount to finding the most effective strategy for your target audience and niche. Experimenting with different approaches is essential to determine what works best for your business. You can try different types of content, promotional strategies, and affiliate programs to see what drives the most traffic and revenue.

By following these steps, you can create an effective affiliate marketing strategy that drives traffic, promotes valuable products, and generates revenue for your business. To attain success in the realm of affiliate marketing, it is crucial to center your efforts on delivering value to your audience and forging a bond of trust and transparency.

Email Marketing

Email marketing is a powerful tool for affiliate marketers, allowing them to communicate directly with their audience and promote relevant products. Here are some tips for effective email marketing:

Build an Email List: The first step in email marketing is to build an email list. Offering a free resource, such as an e-book or webinar, can be an effective method for obtaining email addresses.

Segment Your Email List: To ensure that your emails are relevant and valuable to your audience, you need to segment your email list based on demographics, interests, and behavior.

Use a Reputable Email Service provider: There are many email service providers available that offer a variety of features, such as automation, segmentation, and analytics. Select a reliable provider that caters to your requirements and fits your budget.

Create Valuable Content: Your emails should provide value to your audience. This can include helpful tips, industry news, product recommendations, and special offers.

Use a Clear Call-to-Action: To ensure effective communication, every email should contain a precise call-to-action that motivates the recipient to take a specific action, such as clicking on a link or making a purchase.

Test and Optimize: To improve the effectiveness of your emails, you should test different subject lines, content, and calls to action. Use analytics to track open and click-through rates and adjust your strategy accordingly.

Social Media Marketing

Social media marketing is a vital component of an affiliate marketing strategy as it allows you to reach an extensive audience and promote your products in a more personal and engaging way. To improve your social media marketing, consider these helpful tips:

Choose the Right Social Media Platforms: Many social media platforms are available, but not all are suitable for affiliate marketing. Choose popular platforms among your target audience and allow for affiliate links, such as Facebook, Twitter, Instagram, and Pinterest.

Build a Robust Social Media Presence: Your social media profiles should be professional and consistent with your brand. Use high-quality images, clear descriptions, and relevant keywords to attract and engage your audience.

Post Regularly: Consistency is critical when it comes to social media marketing. Post consistently to keep your audience informed and engaged about your products.

Provide Valuable Content: Your social media posts should provide value to your audience. This can include helpful tips, industry news, product recommendations, and special offers.

Use Visual Content: Visual content, such as videos and images, are more engaging than text-only posts. Use high-quality videos and images to showcase your products and promote your brand.

Engage with Your Audience: Audience engagement on social media requires a two-way conversation, which is crucial for building a connection with them. You must respond to comments and actively foster engagement to create a meaningful connection, ask questions, and participate in relevant conversations.

Use Paid Advertising: Advertising that is paid on social media can help you reach a broader audience and promote your products more effectively. Use targeting marketing options to reach your ideal audience and track your results to optimize your strategy.

Following these tips can create a solid social media presence that drives traffic and sales to your affiliate products.

Paid Advertising

Paid advertising is a powerful tool for affiliate marketers, allowing you to reach a large audience and promote your products more effectively. Here are some tips for effective paid advertising:

Choose the Right Advertising Platform: There are many advertising platforms available, such as Google Ads, Facebook Ads, and Instagram Ads. Choose popular platforms among your target audience and allow for affiliate links.

Set a Budget: Before you start advertising, set a budget you can afford. Test different advertising strategies and adjust your budget accordingly.

Choose a Suitable Ad Format: Different ad formats work better for different products and audiences. Choose ad formats that are engaging, eye-catching, and relevant to your audience.

Target the Right Audience: Use targeting options to reach your ideal audience. Target by demographics, interests, behaviors, and location to ensure your ads are shown to the right people.

Use High-Quality Images and Copy: Your ads should be visually appealing and contain clear, concise copy that promotes your products and brand.

Use Clear Calls-to-Action: It is imperative that each advertisement includes a clear and compelling call-to-action that drives the viewer to take a specific action, such as clicking a link or making a purchase. This is a crucial aspect of effective advertising and should be overlooked.

Test and Optimize: To improve the effectiveness of your ads, you should test different ad formats, copy, and targeting options. Use analytics to track your results, then adjust your strategy accordingly.

Incorporating paid advertising can be a powerful strategy to increase traffic and sales for your affiliate products. By following these tips, you can create compelling ads that reach your ideal audience and promote your products more effectively.

Conclusion

Promoting affiliate products requires a well-planned and executed strategy that encompasses a variety of different channels and tactics. You can increase your reach, engage your audience, and drive more sales by utilizing different ways to promote your affiliate products, such as email marketing, social media marketing, and paid advertising.

To create an effective affiliate marketing strategy, choosing the right affiliate programs, researching your niche, building a website, creating high-quality content, and selecting the right promotional channels for your audience is essential. Focusing on these key elements can create a solid foundation for your affiliate marketing efforts and increase your chances of success.

Email marketing is a preeminent tool for engaging your audience and promoting your affiliate products. By building a targeted email list and sending relevant and valuable content, you can build trust with your audience and drive more sales.

Social media marketing is another effective way to promote your affiliate products. Creating engaging content and building a strong social media presence can reach a wider audience and drive more traffic to your website.

Paid advertising is a powerful tool for driving traffic and sales to your affiliate products. By choosing the right advertising platforms, ad formats, and targeting options, you can create compelling ads that reach your ideal audience and promote your products more effectively.

Incorporating these different promotional channels and tactics into your affiliate marketing strategy can increase your reach, engage your audience, and drive more sales. Remember to regularly test and optimize your strategy to make certain you get the best results possible.

Chapter 7

Tracking and Analyzing Results

How to Track your Affiliate Marketing efforts

Tracking and analyzing your affiliate marketing results is crucial for optimizing your strategy and increasing your earnings. To keep track of your affiliate marketing efforts, follow these steps:

Use Tracking Software: Most affiliate programs provide tracking software that allows you to monitor clicks, conversions, and earnings. This software can provide valuable insights into how well your affiliate marketing efforts are performing and where you can improve.

Set up Google Analytics: Google Analytics is a free tool that can provide detailed insights into your website traffic, along with the number of visitors, where they come from, and what actions they take on your site. You can use this data to track how your affiliate marketing efforts are driving traffic to your website.

Monitor Your Conversion Rate: The conversion rate on your website is the percentage of visitors who complete a specific action, such as making a purchase or subscribing to a newsletter. By monitoring your conversion rate, you can identify which affiliate programs and promotions are most effective and adjust your strategy accordingly.

Use A/B Testing: A/B testing involves testing different versions of your website, landing pages, or promotions to see which performs better. By testing other elements, such as headlines, images, or calls to action, you can optimize your affiliate marketing efforts for maximum effectiveness.

Analyze Your Earnings: Regularly reviewing your earnings can help you identify which affiliate programs and products are most profitable. By focusing on these high-earning programs, you can maximize your profits and improve your overall affiliate marketing strategy.

Review

Tracking and analyzing your affiliate marketing results can help you optimize your strategy and increase your earnings. By using tracking software, setting up Google Analytics, monitoring your conversion rate, using A/B testing, and analyzing your profits, you can gain valuable insights into how well your affiliate marketing efforts are performing and where you can improve.

Tools to Track and Analyze Your Results

There are several tools available to track and analyze your affiliate marketing results. These are a few of the most popular ones:

Google Analytics: Want to learn more about your website traffic and user behavior? Google Analytics offers a free web analytics service that provides in-depth statistics. You can track the number of visitors, their location, the pages they visit, and how long they stay on your site. You can use this information to optimize your affiliate marketing strategy and improve your website's performance.

ClickMeter: ClickMeter is a powerful tracking tool that tracks clicks, conversions, and revenue for your affiliate links. It provides detailed analytics and reporting features that allow you to track your performance over time and identify areas for improvement.

Bitly: Bitly is a link-shortening and tracking tool that allows you to track clicks and analyze link performance. It provides real-time analytics and allows you to create custom links for your affiliate promotions.

Voluum: Voluum is an advanced tracking platform that provides real-time analytics and optimization features for your affiliate campaigns. Allowing you to track clicks, conversions, and revenue for your affiliate links and providing detailed reports and analysis to help you optimize your campaigns.

SEMrush: SEMrush is a comprehensive SEO and marketing analytics tool that provides insights into your website's performance and your competitors. It allows you to track keyword rankings, monitor backlinks, and analyze your website's traffic and user behavior.

These tools can help you track and analyze your affiliate marketing results, optimize your campaigns, and improve your overall performance. Choose the tool that fits your needs and budget, and start tracking your affiliate marketing efforts today.

How to Interpret Data and Make Adjustments

Interpreting data and making adjustments is a crucial aspect of affiliate marketing. These are but a few tips on how to analyze data and make the necessary adjustments to improve your affiliate marketing strategy:

Analyze Your Data: Use your tracking and analysis tools to identify which promotions are performing well and which ones are not. Look at click-through rates, conversion rates, and revenue metrics to understand how your promotions are doing.

Identify Patterns: Look for patterns in your data to help you understand what is working and what is not. For example, certain types of promotions perform better than others, or certain days of the week or times of the day are more effective for promoting your affiliate products.

Experiment with Different Strategies: Use your data to experiment with various promotional strategies. You can conduct a detailed analysis of multiple channels to find the best ways to promote your affiliate products. This can involve using social media, email marketing, or paid advertising to see which methods yield the best results.

Monitor Your Results: Monitor your data to see how your changes affect your performance. Make adjustments and refinements as needed to optimize your campaigns and improve your results.

Continuously Improve: Affiliate marketing is an ongoing process, and it is essential to constantly analyze your data and make adjustments to improve your performance. Use your tracking and analysis tools to monitor your results and make changes as needed to stay ahead of the competition.

By following these tips, you can interpret your data effectively and make the necessary adjustments to improve your affiliate marketing strategy. Remember that data analysis is an ongoing process, and it is essential to continuously monitor your results and make changes as needed to stay competitive in the affiliate marketing industry.

Conclusion

In conclusion, tracking and analyzing your affiliate marketing results is crucial for success in the industry. By using tracking and analysis tools, you can gain insights into your promotional efforts and identify areas where improvements can be made. With this data, you can make necessary adjustments to optimize your campaigns and improve your performance.

Various tools are available to track and analyze your affiliate marketing results, including Google Analytics, affiliate networks' reporting features, and third-party tracking software. These tools allow you to monitor click-through rates, conversion rates, and revenue metrics to understand how your promotions are performing.

Interpreting your data is an essential step in adjusting your affiliate marketing strategy. Analyzing your data for patterns, experimenting with various promotional strategies, and consistently monitoring your results are crucial steps for improving your campaign's performance. Only by doing so can you make informed decisions on optimizing your campaigns. Pay attention to these necessary actions if you want to see real results.

Tracking and analyzing your results is an ongoing process requiring attention and effort. By dedicating time and resources to this aspect of your affiliate marketing strategy, you can achieve long-term success and stay ahead of the competition in the industry.

Chapter 8

Building Relationships with Merchants and Customers

Importance of Building Relationships

Building relationships is a crucial aspect of affiliate marketing because it allows you to establish trust and credibility with both merchants and customers. By fostering positive relationships with these groups, you can increase your chances of success in the industry.

When it comes to merchants, building relationships can help you secure better commissions, gain access to exclusive deals and promotions, and receive personalized support and guidance. Merchants are more likely to work with affiliates they know and trust, so taking the time to build relationships can pay off in the long run.

Similarly, building relationships with customers is crucial because it can lead to increased conversions and repeat business. To establish yourself as a trusted authority in your industry, provide valuable content to your audience, engage with them on social media and via email campaigns, and address their feedback and concerns promptly. Customers will buy a variety of products from you once they *Know, Like and Trust* you. The key to sales.

Building relationships is the cornerstone of building a successful affiliate marketing business. It requires time and effort, but the benefits of establishing trust and credibility with both merchants and customers can lead to long-term success in the industry.

How to Build Relationships with Merchants

The following are some strategies you can use to build relationships with merchants:

Choose the Right Merchants: It's essential to choose merchants whose products or services align with your niche and audience. This makes promoting their products easier and establishing a mutually beneficial relationship.

Reach out to Merchants: Once you've identified potential merchants, reach out to them to introduce yourself and express your interest in promoting their products. Be sure to highlight your relevant experience and audience demographics.

Provide Value: Merchants are more likely to work with affiliates offering value beyond just promotion. Consider ways you can help merchants improve their products or marketing efforts, such as providing feedback or suggesting new promotional strategies.

Stay in Communication: Regular communication with merchants can help build trust and foster a positive relationship. Consider setting up regular check-ins or exchanging updates on promotions and sales.

Attend Events: Attending industry events and conferences can provide opportunities to meet with merchants in person and establish face-to-face connections.

Be Professional: Finally, it's essential to maintain a professional and respectful demeanor when working with merchants. This includes following their guidelines and policies, being transparent about your promotional efforts, and respecting their intellectual property.

How to Build Relationships with Customers

The following are some strategies you can use to build relationships with customers:

Provide Value: The key to building relationships with customers is to provide value beyond just promoting products. This can include sharing helpful tips and advice, providing excellent customer service, and offering personalized recommendations.

Engage with Customers: Engage with your audience on social media, through email marketing, and on your website. Respond to comments, answer questions, and offer support.

Be Authentic: Customers value authenticity and transparency. Be honest about your experiences with products and services, and don't promote products you don't believe in.

Offer Exclusive Promotions: Offer exclusive discounts and promotions to your subscribers and followers. This can help build loyalty and encourage repeat business.

Create Quality Content: Producing high-quality content like blog posts, videos, and social media posts can establish you as an authority/expert in your field and draw in fresh clients.

Use Email Marketing: To stay in touch with your subscribers and customers, use email marketing. Send regular newsletters, product recommendations, and exclusive promotions to keep them engaged.

Ask for Feedback: Ask your customers for feedback on your products and services, which can help you improve your offerings and build trust with your audience.

Remember, building relationships with customers takes time and effort. Focus on providing value, being authentic, and engaging with your audience, and you'll be on your way to building long-term relationships with your customers.

Conclusion

In conclusion, building strong relationships with both merchants and customers is essential for success in affiliate marketing. You can establish trust, increase conversions, and build a loyal following by developing these relationships. To build relationships with merchants, focus on providing value, communicating regularly, and promoting their products in an authentic way. To build relationships with customers, provide value, engage with your audience, and offer exclusive promotions. Building relationships takes time and effort, but the benefits are well worth it in the long run. Your Goal is for them to Know, Like and Trust you and your products.

Chapter 9

Scaling Your Business

How to Scale Your Affiliate Marketing Business

Scaling your affiliate marketing business is about finding ways to increase your revenue and expand your reach. Here are a number of tips on how to scale your affiliate marketing business:

Diversify Your Income Streams: Look for other affiliate programs to promote, consider creating your own products, or explore additional revenue streams such as sponsorships or advertising.

Invest in Paid Traffic: Paid traffic, such as Facebook or Google Ads, can effectively reach a larger audience and increase your affiliate sales.

Build a Team: Consider outsourcing tasks such as content creation or social media management to free up your time and scale your business.

Focus on Automation: Automating specific tasks such as email marketing or social media scheduling can help you scale your business without sacrificing quality.

Develop Partnerships: Find opportunities to collaborate with other affiliate marketers or businesses in your niche, increase your revenue, and expand your reach.

Attend Conferences and Events: Industry conferences and events can help you stay current on the latest trends and connect with potential partners and affiliates. Attend either in person or online.

Remember, scaling your business takes time and effort, but with a solid strategy and the right tools, you can achieve long-term growth and success in affiliate marketing.

Outsourcing and Automation

Outsourcing and automation are two cornerstone strategies for scaling your affiliate marketing business. Here's how you can use them effectively:

Outsourcing:

Identify tasks that take up too much of your time or are not your strong suit, such as content creation, social media management, or customer support.
Look for freelancers or agencies specializing in these tasks with a proven track record.
Develop a clear project scope and expectations for the freelancer or agency and communicate regularly to ensure they meet your needs.
Continuously evaluate the effectiveness of the outsourcing arrangement and make adjustments as needed.

Automation:

Identify tasks that can be automated, such as social media scheduling or email marketing campaigns.
Choose reliable, user-friendly tools that will integrate well with your existing systems.
Develop a straightforward process for implementing automation, including training and testing before full implementation.
Monitor the automation regularly to ensure it functions properly and make adjustments as needed.
Remember that outsourcing and automation are not one-size-fits-all solutions and should be implemented strategically to ensure they are improving efficiency and effectiveness. It is essential to continuously evaluate their impact on your business and make adjustments as needed.

Expanding into New Markets

Expanding into new markets is a key strategy for scaling your affiliate marketing business. Here are some steps to follow when considering expanding into new markets:

Research Potential New Markets: Look at market trends and demographics to identify potential new markets for your affiliate products. Consider factors such as the level of competition, the size of the market, and the purchasing power of potential customers.

Develop a Market Entry Strategy: Determine the best approach for entering the new market, whether it's through organic growth, partnerships with local businesses, or paid advertising.

Adapt Your Content and Promotions: Customize your content and promotional strategies to appeal to the new market. This may involve translating your content into a new language or adjusting your messaging to align with cultural norms and preferences.

Establish Partnerships: Consider partnering with local businesses or influencers to help establish your presence in the new market. By utilizing this, you can expand your customer base and establish credibility with your intended audience.

Monitor and Evaluate: Continuously monitor the performance of your affiliate marketing efforts in the new market. Use analytics to track key metrics and make adjustments as needed to optimize your performance.

Expanding into new markets/niches can be a challenging but rewarding process. By taking a strategic approach and continuously evaluating your performance, you can successfully grow your affiliate marketing business and reach new customers.

Conclusion

In conclusion, scaling your affiliate marketing business can be achieved by implementing various strategies, such as outsourcing and automation, and expanding into new markets. Tactics like these can help you reach a wider audience and increase revenue. It's important to continually analyze and adjust your approach to maximize your efforts and stay ahead of the competition. With dedication and persistence, you can successfully scale your affiliate marketing business and achieve your financial goals.

Chapter 10

Avoiding Common Mistakes

Common Mistakes to Avoid in Affiliate Marketing

There are several common mistakes that affiliate marketers should avoid to ensure the success of their business. Some of these mistakes include:

Choosing the Wrong Niche: Choosing a niche that is too broad or too narrow can hinder your success. Finding a profitable niche that you are passionate about and that has room for growth is essential.

Not Researching Affiliate Programs: Joining affiliate programs requires researching the merchants and their products to avoid promoting low-quality products or those that are not a good fit for your audience.

Not Creating High-Quality Content: Creating content that is not informative or engaging can turn off potential customers and hurt your credibility as an affiliate marketer.

Not Tracking and Analyzing Results: If you keep track of and analyze your efforts, you might be able to understand what's effective and what needs improvement in your affiliate marketing strategy.

Not Building Relationships with Merchants and Customers: Building relationships with merchants and customers is crucial for long-term success in affiliate marketing. Failing to do so can limit your growth and revenue potential.

To increase your chances of success and reach your financial goals in affiliate marketing, it's essential to avoid common mistakes and prioritize building a strong foundation for your business.

How to Avoid Scams

There are several ways to avoid scams in affiliate and or free-lance digital marketing:

Do Your Research: Before you start promoting any affiliate program, research the company and its products/services. Search for reviews and testimonials from other affiliates and customers. Check if the company has a good reputation in the industry.

Check the Terms and Conditions: It's important to carefully review and comprehend the terms and conditions of the affiliate program. Look for any hidden clauses that might put you at a disadvantage. If the terms and conditions appear overly favorable, it's likely that they are not legitimate.

Avoid Programs that require Upfront Payments: Legitimate affiliate programs do not require you to pay any money upfront. If a program asks for an upfront payment, fee, or a deposit, it is likely a scam.

Beware of Pyramid Schemes: Pyramid schemes are illegal and should be avoided. If an affiliate program requires you to recruit new affiliates to make money, it is likely a pyramid scheme.

Use Reputable Affiliate Networks: Affiliate networks provide a layer of protection against scams. They only work with legitimate companies and vet them thoroughly before accepting them into their network.

Trust your Instincts: If something appears too sketchy or too good to be true, it is likely not a reliable program. Trust your instincts and avoid such programs. Avoid the "Shiny Object Syndrome".

Maintaining Ethical Standards

Maintaining ethical standards is an essential aspect of affiliate marketing. While the goal is to generate sales and commissions, it's critical to do so in a way that is honest and transparent.

One important ethical consideration is disclosure. As an affiliate marketer, it is your responsibility to disclose that you are promoting a product and may receive compensation for any sales that come from your promotion. This can be done through a disclaimer on your website or social media accounts.

Another ethical consideration is the quality of the products you promote. It's important only to promote products that you believe in and that you would use yourself. Avoid promoting low-quality products or that may be harmful to consumers.

Finally, the cornerstone of affiliate marketing is maintaining good relationships with merchants and customers. To be reliable, it's essential to address any customer inquiries or concerns promptly and to keep merchants informed of your promotional activities in a transparent manner.

By maintaining high ethical standards, you can build a positive reputation as an affiliate marketer and establish trust with your audience.

Conclusion

In conclusion, avoiding common mistakes and scams and maintaining ethical standards are critical for success in affiliate marketing. To become a successful affiliate marketer, it is essential to avoid mistakes such as promoting low-quality products, spamming, not building relationships, and not tracking and analyzing results. It is also crucial to avoid scams by researching affiliate programs and being cautious of offers that sound too good to be true. It is essential to uphold ethical principles, including disclosing affiliate links and being truthful with customers, to instill credibility and earn the trust of your audience. By avoiding common mistakes, staying vigilant against scams, and maintaining ethical standards, affiliate marketers can establish a successful and sustainable business.

Summary

Making money online through affiliate marketing can be both profitable and adaptable. Nevertheless, just like any other business, it requires thorough planning, strategic thinking, and dedication to achieve success. In this guide, we have provided all the necessary information for you to begin a career as an affiliate marketer. This includes understanding the fundamentals of affiliate marketing, creating and advertising your affiliate website, keeping track of your progress, establishing connections with merchants and customers, expanding your business, and avoiding common errors.

Choosing a profitable niche, researching it thoroughly, and finding the right affiliate programs are crucial steps to success. To boost website traffic and enhance conversions, it is vital to produce high-quality content, optimize it for SEO, and promote it via email marketing, social media, and paid advertising. Analyzing and tracking your results is essential to making informed decisions and adjusting your strategy accordingly. Building relationships with merchants and customers can help you establish trust and credibility, leading to long-term success.

To scale your business, consider outsourcing and automating some tasks or expanding into new markets. However, you should always maintain ethical standards and avoid common mistakes such as promoting low-quality products, spamming, or violating any laws or regulations. This guide provides tips and strategies to help you build a profitable affiliate marketing business that generates passive income and enables you to reach your financial goals.

With continuous learning and improvement, you can achieve success in this field.

Here is a Recap of the Key Points covered in the above material:

Affiliate marketing is a marketing strategy based on performance; an affiliate promotes a merchant's product and earns a commission on any resulting sales.

Choosing a profitable niche is crucial for success in affiliate marketing. Researching your niche can help you identify profitable products and market gaps.

There are various ways to find affiliate programs, including joining affiliate networks, searching on Google, and checking merchant websites.

A website is essential in affiliate marketing, as it provides a platform for creating content and promoting products.

Producing high-quality content for your audience is essential to attract traffic and sales to your affiliate products—quality matters.

Keyword research and SEO can help you optimize your content for search engines and attract targeted traffic to your website.

Promoting affiliate products and boosting website traffic can be achieved through effective social media marketing, email marketing, and paid advertising.

Tracking and analyzing your results using tools such as Google Analytics can help you measure the success of your affiliate marketing efforts and make data-driven decisions.

Building relationships with merchants and customers can help you establish trust and credibility in your niche.

Scaling your affiliate marketing business can be achieved through outsourcing, automation, and expanding into new markets.

It is essential to avoid common mistakes in affiliate marketing, such as promoting low-quality products or failing to disclose affiliate links.

To avoid scams in affiliate marketing, it is vital to research merchants and programs thoroughly and only work with reputable partners.

Maintaining ethical standards, such as providing honest and transparent recommendations, is crucial for building long-term relationships with your audience.

These are just a few of the key points covered in the above material. Affiliate marketing can offer a profitable and fulfilling career if you're willing to invest time and effort in researching your niche, creating top-notch content, and building relationships with merchants and customers. By following the best practices outlined in this material and avoiding common mistakes, you can maximize your chances of success in affiliate marketing.

If you're Considering becoming an Affiliate Marketer, here are some Suggested Steps to take Next:

Choose your Niche: Identify a profitable and interesting niche for which you can create valuable content.

Research and Select Affiliate Programs; Find relevant and high-quality affiliate programs in your niche that align with your values.

Build your Website: Use WordPress to create a professional and user-friendly website, and choose a reliable hosting provider.

Create High-Quality Content: Develop valuable and engaging content that attracts your target audience and promotes your affiliate products.

Promote your Content: Use a combination of email marketing, social media marketing, and paid advertising to reach a wider audience.

Track your Results: Use tracking tools to measure your success, interpret your data, and make adjustments to improve your strategy.

Build Relationships: Connect with merchants and customers to build trust, credibility, and long-term success.

Avoid Common Mistakes: Stay vigilant and avoid scams while maintaining ethical standards.

If you follow these steps and keep learning and adapting, you can achieve success as an affiliate marketer. This business model is both profitable and flexible, offering many benefits.

There are several Benefits of becoming an Affiliate Marketer:

Flexibility: Affiliate marketing allows you to work any time and from anywhere, giving you the flexibility to create your own schedule.

Low Start-up Costs: Affiliate marketing has a low barrier to entry, meaning you can start with minimal investment.

Passive Income Potential: Once you establish your affiliate marketing business and start driving traffic, you can earn passive income from your efforts.

No Need for Inventory or Shipping: As an affiliate marketer, you don't have to worry about keeping inventory or shipping products. The merchant handles all of these tasks.

Unlimited Earning Potential: As an affiliate marketer, you have the possibility/opportunity to earn as much as you want, depending on your efforts and the success of your marketing campaigns.

Skill-Building: Affiliate marketing is a valuable skill that can help you develop digital marketing, sales, and relationship-building expertise.

Networking Opportunities: Affiliate marketing provides opportunities to connect with other marketers and industry experts, expanding your network and learning from others.

Diversification of Income: By promoting multiple products from different merchants, affiliate marketers can diversify their income streams, thus reducing their reliance on a single source of income.

Why Choosing a Niche is Important

Finding a niche is crucial in starting your affiliate marketing journey. By selecting a profitable niche, you can focus on promoting products with high demand and a willing audience. Researching your niche thoroughly, understanding your target audience, and keeping up with industry trends are essential. By following these steps, you can increase your chances of success in affiliate marketing and achieve your goals. Remember, selecting a niche is just the beginning of your journey. It is essential to continue learning and adapting to the evolving market to ensure long-term success.

Next steps for Becoming an Affiliate Marketer

Here is a recap of the key points covered in the above material:

Affiliate marketing entails promoting a merchant's product and earning a commission on any sales made as a result of the promotion. It is a performance-based marketing strategy.

Choosing a profitable niche is crucial for success in affiliate marketing. Researching your niche can help you identify profitable products and market gaps.

There are various ways to find affiliate programs, including joining affiliate networks, searching on Google, and checking merchant websites.

Having a website is essential in affiliate marketing, as it provides a platform for creating content and promoting products.

Creating high-quality content and providing value to your audience is critical for driving traffic and sales to your affiliate products.

Keyword research and SEO can help you optimize your content for search engines and attract targeted traffic to your website.

Promoting affiliate products and increasing website traffic can be achieved through successful email marketing, social media marketing, and paid advertising.

Tracking and analyzing your results using tools such as Google Analytics can help you measure the success of your affiliate marketing efforts and make data-driven decisions.

Building relationships with merchants and customers can help you establish trust and credibility in your niche.

Scaling your affiliate marketing business can be achieved through outsourcing, automation, and expanding into new markets.

It is essential to avoid common mistakes in affiliate marketing, such as promoting low-quality products or failing to disclose affiliate links.

To avoid scams in affiliate marketing, it is crucial to research merchants and programs thoroughly and only work with reputable partners.

Maintaining ethical standards, such as providing honest and transparent recommendations, is crucial for building long-term relationships with your audience.

These are just a few of the key points covered in the above material. Affiliate marketing can be a highly lucrative and rewarding career path for those who put in the effort to thoroughly research their niche, create high-quality content, and forge strong connections with both merchants and customers. By following the best practices outlined in this material and avoiding common mistakes, you can maximize your chances of success in affiliate marketing.

Benefits of Becoming an Affiliate Marketer

There are several benefits of becoming an affiliate marketer:

Flexibility: Affiliate marketing allows you to work any time and from anywhere, giving you the flexibility to create your own schedule.

Low Start-up Costs: Affiliate marketing has a low barrier to entry, meaning you can start with minimal investment.

Passive Income Potential: Once you establish your affiliate marketing business and start driving traffic, you can earn passive income from your efforts.

No need for Inventory or Shipping: As an affiliate marketer, you don't have to worry about keeping inventory or shipping products. The merchant handles all of these tasks.

Unlimited Earning Potential: As an affiliate marketer, you have the opportunity to earn as much as you want, depending on your efforts and the success of your marketing campaigns.

Skill-Building: Affiliate marketing is a valuable skill that can help you develop digital marketing, sales, and relationship-building expertise.

Networking Opportunities: Affiliate marketing provides opportunities to connect with other marketers and industry experts, expanding your network and learning from others.

Diversification of Income: It is imperative for affiliate marketers to broaden their revenue streams and not rely solely on one source of income. This can be achieved by promoting a diverse range of products from multiple merchants.

BONUS CHAPTER

AI IN AFFILIATE MARKETING

Bonus Chapter

AI in Affiliate Marketing

Affiliate marketing is a form of online marketing wherein an affiliate advertises a product or service and receives a commission for each sale. The affiliate typically promotes the product or service through their social media channels, blog, and website. Artificial Intelligence (AI) has become integral to affiliate marketing, providing new opportunities for affiliates and merchants alike. This essay will explore how AI is used in affiliate marketing and its various applications.

Understanding AI

The field of AI in computer science involves developing intelligent machines that can complete tasks typically requiring human intelligence, such as learning, reasoning, perception, and problem-solving. AI is based on the concept of machine learning, which uses statistical algorithms to enable machines to learn from data, identify patterns, and make predictions. AI can be applied in various fields, including healthcare, finance, education, and marketing.

The Role of AI in Affiliate Marketing

AI has transformed the affiliate marketing industry by providing new ways for affiliates and merchants to improve their marketing strategies and increase revenue. Here are some examples of how AI is utilized in affiliate marketing:

Predictive Analytics: Predictive analytics is a form of data analysis that uses statistical algorithms to identify patterns and make predictions about future events. In affiliate marketing, predictive analytics can be used to determine which products or services are likely to sell well based on historical sales data, customer behavior, and other relevant factors. This information can help affiliates and merchants to optimize their marketing strategies and target their audience more effectively.

For example, AI-powered tools such as Affiliate Future and CJ Affiliate can provide predictive analytics based on historical data to predict which products are likely to sell well in the future. This information can help affiliates to choose the right products to promote and merchants to adjust their pricing and marketing strategies.

Natural Language Processing (NLP): NLP is a branch of AI that focuses on the facilitation of computers to understand and process human language. In affiliate marketing, NLP can be used to analyze customer feedback, social media posts, and other sources of customer feedback to understand customer sentiment and identify areas for improvement.

For example, NLP-powered tools such as Brandwatch and Talkwalker can analyze customer feedback on social media platforms to identify trends and insights. This information can help affiliates and merchants better understand their audience and tailor their marketing strategies accordingly.

Chatbots: Chatbots are AI-powered tools that can simulate human conversations and provide customer support and assistance. In affiliate marketing, chatbots can be used to answer customer inquiries, provide product recommendations, and offer personalized promotions based on customer behavior and preferences.

For example, chatbots such as Drift and Intercom can provide personalized recommendations to customers based on their browsing history and purchase behavior. This information can help affiliates and merchants increase customer engagement and drive sales.

Image and Video Recognition: Image and video recognition is a type of AI technology that can analyze images and videos to identify objects, people, and other elements. In affiliate marketing, image, and video recognition can be used to identify products and services in images and videos, enabling affiliates to promote them more effectively.

For example, AI-powered tools like Amazon Rekognition and Google Cloud Vision can analyze images and videos to identify products, logos, and other elements. This information can help affiliates to create more effective marketing campaigns and improve their targeting.

Recommendation Engines: Recommendation engines are AI-powered tools that can analyze customer behavior and preferences, then provide personalized recommendations for products and services. In affiliate marketing, recommendation engines can be used to suggest products and services to customers based on their purchase history, browsing behavior, and other relevant factors.

For example, AI-powered tools such as Amazon Personalize and Refersion can analyze customer behavior to provide personalized recommendations for products and services. This information can help affiliates and merchants to increase customers.

The Role of AI in Free Lance Digital Marketing

Freelance digital marketing is a type of online marketing where individuals offer their marketing services to clients on a contract basis. We provide a diverse array of services, including social media marketing, email marketing, search engine optimization (SEO), content marketing, and other related services. Artificial Intelligence (AI) has become integral to freelance digital marketing, providing new opportunities for freelancers to optimize their marketing strategies and increase their revenue. In this chapter, we will explore the role of AI in freelance digital marketing and its various applications.

Understanding AI: AI is a division of computer science that focuses on creating intelligent machines that can perform tasks that normally require human intelligence, such as learning, reasoning, perception, and problem-solving*. AI is based on the concept of machine learning, which uses statistical algorithms to enable machines to learn from data, identify patterns, and make predictions. AI can be applied in various fields, including healthcare, finance, education, and marketing.

The Role of AI:

AI has transformed the freelance digital marketing industry by providing new ways for freelancers to improve their marketing strategies and increase their revenue. These are some of the ways AI is used in freelance digital marketing:

Personalization: Personalization is vital to digital marketing, allowing marketers to tailor their content and messaging to specific audiences. AI-powered tools can analyze customer data to identify patterns and preferences, enabling freelancers to create personalized content that resonates with their target audience.

For example, AI-powered tools like Marketo and HubSpot can analyze customer data to create personalized email campaigns tailored to specific customer segments. This information can help freelancers to increase engagement and drive conversions.

Search Engine Optimization (SEO): SEO is the technique of optimizing websites to achieve a rank higher in search engine results pages (SERPs). AI-powered tools can analyze search engine algorithms and customer behavior to identify the most effective SEO strategies.

For example, AI-powered tools such as SEMrush and Moz can analyze search engine data to identify keywords and content strategies that are most likely to drive traffic and conversions. This information can help freelancers to optimize their clients' websites and improve their search engine rankings.

Social Media Marketing: Social media marketing involves promoting services and products through social media platforms like Facebook, Twitter, and Instagram. AI-powered tools/devices can analyze social media data to identify trends and insights, enabling freelancers to create more effective social media campaigns.

For example, AI-powered tools such as Hootsuite and Sprout Social can analyze social media data to identify the most effective content and messaging strategies for specific audiences. This information can help freelancers to increase engagement and drive conversions on social media platforms.

Content Marketing: Content marketing involves creating and sharing high-quality content to attract and retain customers. AI-powered tools can analyze customer data to identify the most effective content strategies.

For example, AI-powered tools such as ContentStudio and BuzzSumo can analyze customer data to identify the most popular topics and formats for specific audiences. This information is useful for freelancers who want to create engaging content that connects with their desired audience.

Chatbots: Chatbots are AI-powered tools that can simulate human conversations and provide customer support and assistance. Chatbots are often used to answer customer inquiries, provide product recommendations, and offer personalized promotions based on customer behavior and preferences.

For example, chatbots such as ManyChat and Tars can provide personalized recommendations to customers based on their browsing history and purchase behavior. This information can help freelancers to increase customer engagement and drive sales.

Predictive Analytics: Predictive analytics is a form of data analysis that uses statistical algorithms to identify patterns and make predictions about future events. In freelance digital marketing, predictive analytics can be used to identify which marketing strategies are likely to be most effective for specific audiences.

*What Is Artificial Intelligence? - Rebellion Research.
https://www.rebellionresearch.com/what-is-artificial-intelligence

Summary

The role of AI in freelance digital marketing is significant and offers numerous benefits to freelancers in optimizing their marketing strategies and enhancing their revenue. Artificial Intelligence (AI) is a field of computer science that empowers machines to carry out tasks that generally necessitate human intelligence, such as learning, reasoning, perception, and problem-solving. In the realm of freelance digital marketing, AI is applied in various ways to revolutionize the industry.

Firstly, AI enables personalized marketing by analyzing customer data and identifying patterns and preferences. Through the use of customized content and messaging, freelance digital marketers can successfully establish a connection with their intended target market, leading to a rise in audience interaction and, ultimately, greater conversion rates. AI-powered tools like Marketo and HubSpot can use customer data to create personalized email campaigns, helping freelancers to deliver more targeted and effective marketing campaigns.

Secondly, AI is crucial in search engine optimization (SEO). By analyzing search engine algorithms and customer behavior, AI-powered tools like SEMrush and Moz can identify effective SEO strategies, helping freelancers optimize their clients' websites and improve search engine rankings. This leads to increased visibility and organic traffic for their clients' businesses.

Thirdly, social media marketing is transformed by AI. Hootsuite and Sprout Social are AI-powered tools that analyze social media data. They help freelancers to create more effective social media campaigns by identifying trends and insights. By understanding customer behavior and preferences, freelancers can tailor their content and messaging to specific audiences, driving engagement and conversions on social media platforms.

Additionally, AI enhances content marketing by analyzing customer data and identifying popular topics and formats for specific audiences. Tools like ContentStudio and BuzzSumo provide insights that help freelancers create valuable and relevant content that resonates with their target audience. This enables freelancers to attract and retain customers through effective content marketing strategies.

Chatbots, another AI application, play a vital role in customer support and assistance. Chatbots like ManyChat and Tars simulate human conversations and can answer customer inquiries, provide recommendations, and offer personalized promotions based on customer behavior and preferences. This improves customer engagement and drives sales for freelancers' clients.

Lastly, AI-powered predictive analytics helps freelancers identify effective marketing strategies for specific audiences. By analyzing data and patterns, predictive analytics tools enable freelancers to make informed decisions and predict future marketing outcomes. This helps in optimizing marketing strategies and driving better results for clients.

Conclusion

In conclusion, the role of AI in freelance digital marketing is transformative, offering freelancers new opportunities to enhance their marketing strategies and drive better results for their clients. AI-powered tools enable personalized marketing by analyzing customer data and tailoring content and messaging to specific audiences, leading to increased engagement and conversions. AI also plays a crucial role in SEO, helping freelancers optimize websites and improve search engine rankings, resulting in greater visibility and organic traffic. Social media marketing is elevated by AI, providing insights and trends that enable freelancers to create more effective campaigns on social media platforms. Additionally, AI enhances content marketing by identifying popular topics and formats, allowing freelancers to create valuable and relevant content. Chatbots powered by AI provide customer support and assistance, improving customer engagement and driving sales. Lastly, predictive analytics aids freelancers in making informed decisions and predicting marketing outcomes. Embracing AI in freelance digital marketing empowers freelancers to deliver targeted, data-driven strategies that yield tangible results for their clients. As AI advances, its impact on freelance digital marketing will only grow, creating new possibilities for freelancers to thrive in the ever-evolving digital landscape.

www.ingramcontent.com/pod-product-compliance
Lightning Source LLC
Chambersburg PA
CBHW062359290526
45794CB00003B/1007